IF
LOVE
HAD A
NAME

davina@alegriamagazine.com

Ordering Information:
Quantity sales. Special discounts are available on quantity
purchases by corporations, associations, and others. For
details, contact the publisher at
davina@alegriamagazine.com

Orders by U.S. trade bookstores and wholesalers. Please
contact Big Distribution:
www.ingramspark.com

Printed in the United States of America.

Library of Congress Control Number: 2020911947

ISBN: 978-1-7347252-3-0

Cover design: Tania Peregrino
Book design: Diana & Omar Castañeda
Sirenas Creative

Con mucho
cariño,
Para: Jessie
Medina ♡,

Davina F.

IF **LOVE** HAD A NAME

poems by Davina Ferreira

ALEGRIA
PUBLISHING

Acknowledgements

I want to thank The Community Literature Initiative (CLI) & professor Hiram Sims for his mentorship.

I also want to thank my love, Andrew Altman for sharing me with my art - not an easy task- and for being my #1 supporter. Your love has allowed me to keep growing into the woman I am today.

Foreword

*"Love is just a mirror,
pointing me to my own
direction."*

I am raising five daughters. Five beautiful, brilliant little ladies who desperately long to be women. They melt crayons to create make-up, they get dressed up as doctors and teachers, they put balloons underneath their shirts and pretend they are pregnant. They wear braids and beads in their hair while stealing high heels from their mother's closet and walking around the house-practicing. Little girls, juggling childhood in their palms, longing to be grown women. I am raising them, and I don't know what I'm doing. When they were born, I said to their mother, "All my life, I have dreamed of manhood. How can I teach them how to be women?' She said, "You won't have to, but you can teach them how a man should love a woman by the way you love me."

If Love Had a Name is an outstanding collection of poems centered around real womanhood. It is a lyrical whirlwind of self-love, independence, and the courage a woman needs to explore the world without a man holding her hand and leading her through it. Davina has gathered up every ounce of womanly pride necessary to stand on her two strong feet and placed it here between these pages. A poetry book is a collection of poems, and a collection is defined as "an accumulation of objects gathered for study, comparison, or exhibition." I encourage you to study these poems, compare these poems to your own experience, and let them be a divine exhibition of what it means to honor women, and celebrate their independent power.

"Tides breaking within and sunsets sliding under my feet:
Every living moment where tranquility is offered: take it.
It is a gift from your creator."

Poetry is the way I can hear what God wants to say to me. I have been lectured to, preached to, coached, counseled, and mentored. But when something I need to hear is written in a poem, I can hear it clearly. When I read this book, I heard God saying to me, "Women are valuable. They are my greatest creation-vessels by which abundant life enters into this world. Their life is a gift to them, not just a gift to you. I did not create them for the purpose of serving you. I created them for the purpose of serving Me." I am sure you will have your own experience and you thumb through these pages, and while you do, listen to the creator has to say to you.

"A woman's heart may take long to get it right,
but once it does,
you'd better know
it's out of your control. "

Hiram Sims
The Community Literature Initiative

This book is dedicated to every young girl, woman, & womXn awakening with me at this very moment.

THIS IS NOT THE LOVE POETRY BOOK YOU WILL

open up,
mark up page by page,
highlight in bright pink
after drying up your tears
with a box of tissue paper.

This is not the love poetry book
where Neruda compares you to the
brightest sun
Nor
It is a tale of impossible love.

If that's what you thought,
I may have to refund you,
or give you some credit.

This book is my own love story
A creator's gamble
An ode to my own heart
as my savior,

This book es un himno
To my womanhood
Mi feminidad

A hat
the wind does not blow away,
A bunch of flowers from all the
days I did not give

True
    Love
        To myself

This is not the love poetry book
where Romeo dies with you,
because he was not even invited.

I ask myself instead
to chill that sparkling wine,
to sit outside and watch the stars.

Play with my own dreams
as loving confessions
Bathe myself in the river
of truth

Unmask my limitations
Celebrate my inclinations

Revel in my beauty
as a way to true
Liberation

This book is not charming
prince
at the table
Instead
I pushed him over a cliff
And told him:
You should learn to truly live.

This book es un himno
To my womanhood
Mi feminidad

A hat
the wind does not blow away,
A bunch of flowers from all the
days I did not give

True
    Love
        To myself ....

THEY CALLED ME
P
U
T
A

She is just going to be like her mother,
get pregnant by 17

Instead I went
and I got a life
you would not believe.

Yes,
men chased me more
than I could handle,
a perfect recipe for trouble.

Alone in a new country,
naive desde mi raíz
no parents around to smell
men's intentions,

and my heart too young to
understand the implications.

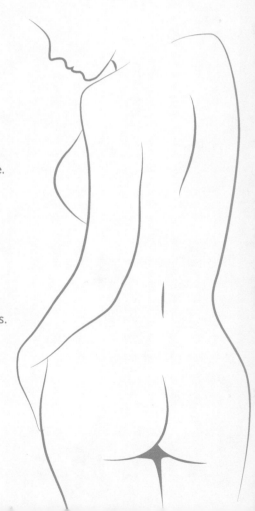

They called me Puta
because my beauty
scared
certain
lovers & family members,
so they slut shamed me,

made themselves feel
above me,
with their crooked moral
compasses.

This is the problem:
when you tell a young girl she is a puta,
when she is just learning about herself,

when she is just making sense of her own
power,
she begins to give her power away
to everyone she thinks will see it.

Looking for it in the wrong places,
including strangers,

she longs for a new home,
before she knows she is her own

Home

That girl you call a puta,
perra,
slut,
zorra
 will begin to believe it,
hate herself as she dives deeper,

self-destruction
 without
instructions,

hit rock bottom
take years to come to terms
with all it could have been of herself,
if she did not waste so many years
finding love in awful places.

But don't feel pity
It does get better

This Puta,
Went to college &
graduated with honors,
lifted herself out of poverty,

made all the mistakes

the so called putas make,
dated the wrong men,

But at the end,
she found herself.
Crowned her inner self,

Her heart
her greatest treasure,

a castle with many rooms
for forgiveness

a palace of words
long forgiven.

She no longer looks for that home.
She knows now,

She is her own

HOME
&
She is worth of having it all.

HOW MUCH DOES KINDNESS COSTS IN TODAY'S WORLD?

Same as a Starbucks lattè
or a little more?

I mean those nice good mornings you
envision in small towns,
where once upon a time
the human mind
depended on each other's smiles

Now,
 Kindness has raised its whole-sale price,
its import export rates
plus inflation
that gives it an extra jump
in today's
economic relations

But how about thinking in terms of free
trade,
 lifting our faces we can remember to
say
HELLO
Buenos Días
Bon Jour

....

(Fill in your language)

How much does kindness costs in
today's world ?

More than a happy meal,
a new Gucci belt,
a Supreme backpack ,
Instagramable photos,
Boomerangs,
Tik toks,
Everything LIVE

I say
Let
kindness
be that gate to each other's hearts
A first-class priority
You can set the tone
for a new, more compassionate world

Face to face,
Hand to hand
Human to human.

Don't let kindness cost you a thing.

Give it freely.

Hold that heavy door for someone,
let the one who seems more tired than you
take your seat,
Look at everyone that helps you during the
day and ask

How are you?

 And mean it

Notice them

Make them feel they matter

Because they do.

You do.

Don't let kindness cost you a thing.

Sit with your pain,
Ask for its full name,
Prepare a cup of tea
for her/him
&
face to face
between sips
make
your presence
soothe its fear.

WHERE I COME FROM...

The rain is beautiful,
The air smells of
a thousand flowers,
Trees are the brightest green
you will ever see.

Where I come from
Familia is everything,
Money is only complementary.

People laugh
even if they had a bad day
&
if they don't know
where
their next meal is coming from,
they still smile & make jokes.

That's how people are
where I come from.

Donde comen 2 comen 4

Where 2 can eat 4 can indeed.

At the store,
if you have not gotten paid,
they let you open up a tab to
pay later,
and if you are broke
your bestie will get you.

Where I come from...

The rain is beautiful,
Nature speaks to you
ancestral truths
and
God lives closer.

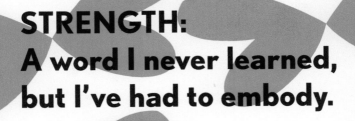

STRENGTH:
A word I never learned,
but I've had to embody.

NOWADAYS

Tears may have flown
in lonesome rivers
But now,
 the sea crystalizes them
into ponds of golden sand,

A waking sun in the tropics,
Hips wide,

Nowadays,
Self-love is my super power.

I may not be able to take back
the time I gave you,
But I am now writing my own
Historia.

You are perfect
as you are.

Impeccable as moon light
and stardust

(Don't let anyone convince you otherwise)

17

I was 17 when
I left Medellin with my suitcase
full of dreams,
put myself on a flight to the unknown,
and defied the odds.

Sat alone at recess
with the only 2 Spanish speakers,
made the line with
disabled children.

Ate the free tuna with saltines
for low income students,
walked 40 minutes to school.

And on my way home
discovered quesadillas,
found .50 cent donuts for self-love
and one friend who
 was more than enough.

I wrote depressing journal entries in diaries.
I became a friend
of the dictionary.

Back then.
Going back home was out
of the question.

You are an Artist

My first American boyfriend
was the one
who helped me understand,
who I really was

one afternoon
before I went to bootcamp,
to become a U.S marine.

I thought it would be
my only way to
pay for college.

He grabbed me by my hand
as we sat on a sidewalk
on Beach Blvd
and told me:

-You are an artist,
the military life is not for you-

The next day
I took my stuff from
 where I used to stay,
signed my resignation,
wondered if

my first winter would be
too long,

I did not know
if I could survive at 18
on my own.

He made sure
I found a safe place
to write
and study.

I borrowed an old bicycle,
worked as a hostess,
enrolled at a community college.

The seeds of my dreams
got planted.

One day
he left
to go travel through Africa,
found himself a wife and many
children.

I remember
how much I cried
when I saw him
leaving

His kind heart
saw in me
what others didn't,

even if he did not speak Spanish
& I did not speak English.

Ever since then,
I believe in angels.
They truly
show up
when you need them.

LOVE SEEKER

Seeking in you
what I lack in myself,
I go deep into my longing.
How your love would remedy
any ache and pain
I feel.

But little did I know,
you came here to merely
show me
that my love lacks its most
important direction.
That it has lost its course.
That it runs astray
all on its own.

Looking where there are not
answers to be grasped like
dew in peaceful mornings.

Love is just a mirror,
pointing me to my own
direction.

A rare,
but perfect intersection
where my soul can dream
of its own reflection.

GOD'S LOVE

Te Amo,
You say it
Every day

You show me "it"
Every day

Your love walks around my heart
Como un día de sol

And I don't take it for granted.

My Accent

My accent is a song that can make you sway,
 dance or laugh,

Let me tell you about my pride,
Colombian
American

Spanish from Medellín,
and English from my Californian dreams.

 My accent is a song,
which reminds me every day
where I come from.

 This strong accent,
Sweet,
Enticing,
Slow,

B I G
U L
z
G

 and sometimes phonetically wrong
but
It lets my heritage crawl back on my soul
and I don't want to let it go:

Call it nostalgia of lost loves,
of Ancestral memories -long gone,
of Grandmother's orchids' scent
and green mangos under the sun.

My accent is a song that can make you
undress and calm your nerves,

A cadence of songs played long ago,
melodies of days forever gone by
 -that come back to me today,
and remind me
De Donde Vengo yo.
Where I come from.

 But, don't be deceived:
I did go to school and I may even write a little better than you.

R   T   K   D   H   P

And though I may look fair,
 I carry within me the Amazon and the conquistador,
the tortured and the executioner.
I carry them all.

Indigenous in my love of nature,
native & wild as a rare flower.
The African in me loosens her hips
when she listens to that Salsa beat,
and the Portuguese
reminds me of the grandfather,
 I am still to meet.

Remembrance of times long forgotten.
A consciousness to transcend what was done before
as I seek to return one day to my essential,
 truthful wholeness.

My accent is my song and it reminds me everyday,
 Where I come from,
De donde vengo yo.

Was it Worth it?

If you ask me
if it was worth the pain
of not seeing my parent's age,
living abroad,
to embark out on my own,

to build empires of hope
in a place so unknown,
I would tell you:

I don't quite know,
most days I am glad
 I have flown
over the weight
 of my own limited outlook
of the world
where I had grown,
but others days, I do wonder

If you are an immigrant,
If you once abandoned everything and everyone you loved,
then you know.

Was it worth it?
The new house and monthly mortgage?
The dream of "freedom" as stardom?
The chasing and the getting?
The accolades and the sound of nearby fortune?

You tell me.
Mi Hermano,
Mi hermana
Emigrante.

Was it worth the pain,
the bleeding profits,
the nights of terror and consolation?
The testing of your own self - will and power?

If you ask me,
 I can tell you.
A good thing is:
 I learned to fly
 beyond my limits-
saw deadly fear
 and crushed it
with my own fingers.
Exchanged my certainty
for limitless,
became a delusional dreamer,
 learned the value of a day's work,
prayed in gratitude,
 humbled.

You tell me.
Mi Hermano,
Mi hermana
Emigrante.

Listen to your corazón.

What better love
that the one
who holds you
through it all.

GODDESS

She looks at herself in the mirror
and does not see her ancient halo.

She has been beaten & broken.
She has lost her memory of greatness.

That is, until she cleans her wounds
over many moons & slowly caresses
herself through tears and laughter.

BROKEN

As an old door
no one cares to fix,
you came in and
left it
as you found it.

You did not care
to see if my heart

still had
a chance to heal.

CAHUENGA BLVD.

26 Never looked so good.
Red salsa dancing dress & lace underwear,
118 pounds, no cellulite,
confidence in her walk.
She knows with one look
she can get any man she wants.

Cheap Chardonnay in her
Old Hollywood gritty apartment
1920's beautiful windows.

The Hollywood sign to her backside.
and
out on the Blvd of the stars
where the action lies,
Thai food under $10 dollars
and a handsome stranger.

A perfect Thursday evening.

Cahuenga Blvd.
A homeless man lays on the ground,
like

she would
in Griffith Park some years ago,

She passes by with her 5 inch heels and tries not to wake him.

Then, she goes down on to the Hollywood stars and steps on them,
dreaming like a million and 1 girls,

/One day one will be mine/

Trust me,
You don't want to be stepped on.

That café in the corner,
where
everyone is dreaming,
until it's time for lunch and the last 20 dollars are gone.

What will we eat tomorrow?
We could not live on art alone.

The smell of weed and pee and that sweet,
 strange air of possibility
 or
 delusion

Cahuenga Blvd.
Someone passes by.
Are they happy or are they high?

No time to waste.
She is 26,
trying to see what she can get,
making love twice a night,
and sometimes even in the light of day.

Hollywood
the city of stars,
has so many tales to tell
a million dreamers hustling away.

Broke?
Maybe today is her lucky break

Cahuenga Blvd.
Love making when that's all you really have.
When that's all you think you can give.

YOUR LOVE

Like a miracle I never thought possible,
you appear to give me the world
for no other reason than Being ME.
I wonder,
Is there a trick?

I am not used to getting so much like this:
-Anything you want -you say,

-You are as beautiful as I last remember you-
I chose to believe you.
I can just BE.

Why did it take me so long to KNOW that I am enough?

Never did I think:
Being ME
        would be a quality alone,
his love encompassing it all,
reminding me,
I am made of
            Beauty.

GIVE ME

Love as Medicine.
Freedom as Love.

Give me

Libertad

como

Amor.

TRUTH

Just in case someone tells you
What love is.

Close your eyes and touch your own heart,
Distinguish its magic beat.

Its unique melody and cadence.

IF LOVE HAD A NAME

It would be
sunny mornings in the countryside,
Green Mango con limón & sal.
Eating it with my hands
at my grandmother's farm.

Fresh squeezed orange juice from my
mother's hands,
Baby brothers running about
laughing around.

If love had a name,
It would be
Salsa dancing at 23,
singing at church by 7 or 8.
Prayers answered,
hope never faltering.

It would be open-hearted conversations,
no expectations,
being able to get to know the other &
having hot tea with honey.

My father's salads on Sundays.
 Immigrant's hands.
Year after year
of Western Union wires,
even when you don't have the money.

If love had a name,
and a physical address,
It would be 30 houses long
where I have lived, and sought
to find my real home.

Its doors as suitcases,
dreams manifested,
nothing like that feeling
of enduring it all
to one day make it.

It would be your strong hands
supporting me.
It would have your lips
as fleshy pillows.

It would hold an eternity of sounds and syllables,
drums of silence &
a wild caress in the Caribbean.

If love really had a name,
it would be a newborn's gaze,
divine presence
always hiding even though is present.

It would also include:
books,

dogs
a fireplace
two suitcases
a new world around the corner
a hand always extended.

Unplanned laughter
an adventure or two
a hot lover or two
an open plan
a soft pen
trees
&
colorful flowers

Best friends for each theme & occasion
of all races and creeds,
vibrating together.

Its name would include
poetry as my way of living
and also, my unborn children.

If love had a name
it would have to be
imperfect parents
around the corner
not too far & not so near,
but always present.

It would be grandmother holding 3 jobs to take care of 7.

Fresh Avocado,
Fried Plantains,
Chips and Salsa.

Falling in love with a stranger,
Silk & Lace dresses,
meeting you,
sleeping next to you.

If love had a better name

It would be

WOMAN

WomXn

Goddess

DIOSA.

A HANDSOME
STRANGER

Like in the fairy tales,
his blue eyes
find yours
and his hand grabs
your heavy suitcase
before it falls down
an escalator.

You have your hands full,
and he prevents you
from falling.

There is not a word
Exchange-
only a gaze of kindness.

A rare gentleman
you will never see again

and you wonder
as a naive romantic

if he will take the same train,
follow you to your seat,

and tell you the meaning of life
in three words
with his clothes off.
&
you will find your purpose
in everything he states
without having to do all
your inner work.

Then his body
 would remind you

how easy you can get lost in
the dreams of someone
as fatally removed from reality
as a beautiful stranger.

I get on the train,
and right behind me

the door closes
 with my own erotic fantasies
as a quick fixation

and a new protagonist
to my story,

which now has one
Irreplaceable heroine,
one which carries
 her own
heavy suitcase
down escalators,
one that gives kindness
first to herself

and finds her purpose
in the gift of living
feeling freely an
Empowered woman,
A lover to herself
First.

you

You are the problem I crave and don't need,

the disordered way I could turn my life upside down,
desire at its knees,
delayed prayer,
messy hair entangled en tu piel.
 Chaotic dreams,
a secret evening of sins
I dream.

You are the problem I
I crave.
Wild lovemaking,
white cotton bedsheets &
palm trees,
sexy conversations,
no domestication.

Can a wild woman
ever be caged?

Or will she dilute in your palm like water?

Dreams of serene,
 dangerous Liberty.

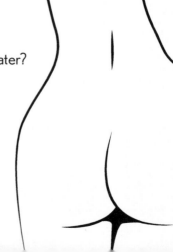

DELICIOUS

Imagining
how delicious it would be to taste you as a new exotic dish,
slowly
taking you all in,
moans, sighs and bites,
all of it until I clean my palate
fully satisfied.
Then a few seconds later
ready for dessert,
kissing every layer which makes you so bittersweet,
exquisitely dangerous,
sour like green mango with salt & Lemon,
earthy like root vegetables & sandalwood.
Sweet like raw honey,
rare like a mix of sweet berries & reishi mushrooms.

A potion.
A recipe for madness and dependency,
A never-ending night of carnal desires,
tasting you as I look at you,
as I lick my own lips,
Wet as water

As I observe what's next to devour:
YOU,
All of you!

I would begin with your lips,
  A savage little squeeze,
then slowly my tongue
rolling in,
fork in hand,
your mouth hot as as oven.

Then sliding down your neck,
inhaling your addicting manly scent,
as I wonder how long it will take to have my full meal all to myself.

Desire is a hungry animal.

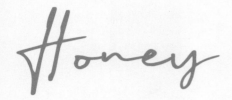 

I have forgotten my own
honey
given to me
by creation

strawberry
dipped
Chocolate

No one
to steal my pleasure

No one
to pleasure
but my dreams

Nor
make it hurried
dutiful
but
pure
creation

A special gift
from me
to
myself

How about my own
PLEASURE?

How's that

For

Reclaiming
what's mine

No one
to colonize

Feminine
Freedom

My lips
tasting their own

a sacred body
that
smiles,

Gasps for air

Gives itself
a new
kind
of
climax

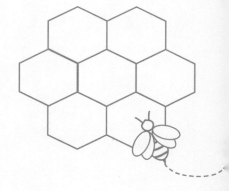

Finally,
Flying

That's what I'm
talking about

You get me?

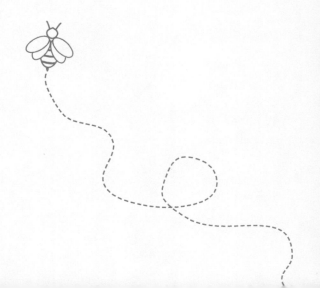

WHEN WE AWAKEN

No matter how much
I love you,
my heart has an agenda of its own.

It finally walks the talk.
Talks the walk.

No drama necessary.
Its theatre doors are all closed.

Perhaps just an echo of an opening line,
a rehearsed dance behind closed curtains,
but all of it unnecessary.

You see,
my heart now has its own home.
Walks naked on its own.
Orders room service
& sips tea in the afternoon.

None of the past karmas,
 a low tolerance zone.

You came in to love?

You are welcome.

You came to hate?
You are on your own.

A woman's heart may take long to get it right,
but once it does,
you'd better know
it's out of your control.

-you are just an option-

She is finally happy on her own.

I learned that love
sleeps not in the deep sea,
but at every shore.

I learned that love
lives not in the greed
Of tomorrow,

But at the peak of
my present moment.

YOUTH

Self-love can't be traded off
Listen,
hear it from an older sister:

Smarts will beat fillers
any day of the week.
Enter that room,
believe in you own grace.

A smile will do more than silicone
& compassion will make you
stand tall.

Kindness will always
win
you
real followers

if that's what you think will go
down in history.

I said

Hear it from an older sister:
Heartbreak shall pass
 as Botox injections.

Cultivate your dreams and
passions,
Take care of your relationship with your
Higher power

At the end,
Remember there is nothing to take.
Everything you give will be
your only way to truly stay.

Motherhood

To be a mother or not to be,
That is the question,
I ask myself.

Some friends say
 that giving birth is to die and be reborn again.

A new woman is born;
the old one gets shredded.
Gone as her old loves archived under her broken bones.

Scars all around,
stiches up and down.
Her sacred body stretched out,
nipples tortured.

Then,
you see your baby's face
 and you realize someone
 just became your very life
(and perhaps your own death).

You have never loved ANYONE that way?

To be a mother or not to be...
One must die to taste the sweetest of all loves.

- "The greatest of them all."
they say.

A deeper love that I have never felt before

But to die again?

Am I willing to agonize once more for that one great love?

I'm tired of dying now.

I'm finally living.

Now,
 that I am finally walking on my own womanly sky,
creating my victory with prideful strides,
a muse to myself
 at last.

Finally accepting of my gifts and my curves,
Fully and unapologetically a

     WOMAN.

To be a mother or not to be...

Sometimes I fantasize when strollers pass me close by.
 I imagine his red hair and light grandmother's eyes,
a dreamy smile
I seem to grasp from another lifetime.

But a bit too quickly,
I go back to my
daily thinking:

Libre como el viento!

Free like the wind!

A woman at times must choose to be a mother
or to keep her course.

Put away on a shelf,
 whatever she creates,
 at least for some time,
the magic of love will get them reawakened.

To be a mother or not to be...
Judge me if you may,
As women, we have now that right
-To be conscious mothers or no mothers at all-

Count your blessings
and become like
La luna.

It shines bright
& awaits in its
light
a miracle.

You are blessed like no other.

Look around you.

WHEN ARE YOU HAVING A BABY?

"When are you having a baby?"

How about you mind your own business?

Like if it was a woman's only destiny
to give birth to a human life
as if it was a snap your fingers
kind of decision.
As if she knew God's plans.

I am going to be a mother

Cuando Dios quiera,
- I said-

Which means,
When it's God's will.

If you must know
Yes,
I have asked for divine intervention,
signs and visions,
answers through dreams & subliminal messages
to know
if I am wrong for even giving it
a second thought.

Let's say so far the answer has been this:

live your dreams, enjoy a season of well - deserved peace,
write that-book, tour it, live it, share it with other women, help
orphaned children, travel, volunteer, read to kids, get to share
more time with your own mother, produce that film you have
been thinking about for years, go back to the stage, learn French,
be good to yourself, be kind to others always.

So far,
this has been God's latest answer.

ODE TO SELF-LOVE

You are infinity
Dressed up in borrowed clothes,
the Milky Way in every act of hope,

You are
the aroma of a rose's silent scent,
Dew in the mornings,

A new moon in every hope
you silently carry

You are
The wild dance of the ocean,
the brilliance of golden sand,
mystery disguised in every child.

Grace for breakfast,
a collection of miracles
threaded together.

You are
collective sorrow & unexplainable laughter,
Someone to live for

A creator's beloved

You are
that
SOMEONE
you don't remember,
the one at times you ignore,
the one you should hug.

A hundred blessings

You are your first love,
the butterflies in the stomach you thought
 were because
of the "other."

You are
the generous heartbeat
that loves you,
until this earth erodes you.

You are the reason
someone lost their sleep,
& found their true dream,

You are the result of endless hours
A twisted mystery of metaphysics and biology,
A smile for someone in
desperation.

You are
the one the sun wakes up to
No questions asked
Sins forgiven,

A new butterfly learning about migration,
a wild wave in a deserted island

You are infinite,
the aroma of a rose's silent presence,

Dew in the mornings,
a new moon in every hope
you silently carry.

Our love

we give to each other
as calming medicine.

BEAUTIFUL DAYS

Even beautiful days can have windy strikes;
Do not let them get less beautiful than they
are.

Beautiful days have a certain
easy – floating kindness
 easing into smiles,

A stranger's hello
 sparkling
a new hope
 once lost.

Beautiful days can be as rare or
 as continually surprising as you let them:
a warm heart under your coat,
a tender way to salute an aching brother or
sister's heart.

Beautiful days are gifts,
gigantic stars filled with gratitude
and some heroic sort of glory.

Beautiful days.
Let them sink in.

You are worth it.
All of them,

Divine Child.

I AM

All is here in this unperceived
breathable moment of self

I float in everything that was,
that is and
that will always be.

A grain of sand divided in a thousand
colors,
Futile,
 yet
 all knowing.

Close your eyes and breathe
eternity in God's favor.

The rest,
these images are pure illusion.

Somewhere among the mirrors,
there is a soul waiting to be rescued from
division,
seeking wholeness.

I AM.
Love All Embracing.

Totality in every heartbeat.

All embracing Love.

What you believe to be your biggest ABISMO,
Awaits for you as sacred wisdom.

Walk with me
to the closest mountain
of your true self
& peek within:

Salty roots of
dreams undreamed

Waiting for you
to drink your
own healing potion.

PEACE

Hold your heart
with both hands
&
feel its melody.

A sacred home lives
within you,
your breath its roof,
your love its destiny.

Let peace come and
sit for breakfast,
offer it tea &
Let it sip
calm into your
heart.

TRANSFORM

You can't bathe in
the same river twice
-says the wise.

Surrendering
to the Creator
of all things

fleeting dreams
You and me

Transformed

An ever-changing
masterpiece.

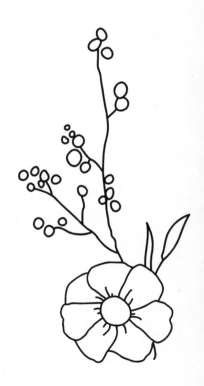

DIVORCE

A call you never forget.
Your heart splits open
Yet miraculously,
 it does not
bleed until one day
you grow up
and remember:

I lost my home.
My country.
My parent's dreams,
Their golden years.

-Your parents are getting divorced.
Where do you want to live?-

And they call themselves adults
asking a child what her destiny means.

You hang up the phone,
Put on red lipstick at 7,
ignore the fact
It hurts you at all.

You go out to play.
Put on an oversized sweater
Get lost in imaginary worlds
until one day

You finally get it.

MY MOTHER

She has the seven lives of a cat.
Robbed, kidnapped for a night
thrown from a bus.
She had three brain surgeries on the same day,
woke up like new the next night.

She dreams of being like Coco Chanel,
becoming a star in the last years of her life,

May she design the life she wants
Begin from scratch
Everyone deserves a second chance.

My mother is a muse-
her own galaxy of pain and beauty,
Laughter and tears.
The longing for a sunny day in a heavy night.

CHOSEN

You were 19.

You became my stepmother,
Madrastra
A name
 you dislike
to this day.

And that's right:

You deserve the name of the sky,
a full life of sun light,
all the green of the mountains.

You accepted me.

I came with the package,
and you took me under your wings
Cared for me
when I was sick

Helped me
in times
 when life got
rock bottom
 tragic

When hope
sky- dived faster
 than my
inner power.

You were there.
Never a question.

I have since
stopped naming you.

How do you name the one who saves a child?

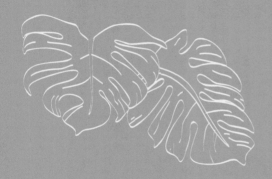

GREEN MANGOS

If you want to know who I am,
look for me in the memory of tall mango trees.

PARIS

When it rains in Paris,
dreams float in the air.
Tear drops of rain become poetry
& a recollection of every love once loved and lost
stops by.

When it rains in Paris,
I say - forgive me lovers-
my soul is free with Libertad,
fully awaken to my womanhood.

When it rains in Paris,
I,
Ecstatic in my loneliness,
I,
Bliss at every corner
I,
Lips forged with words of power,
I,
My best romance,
I,
Finally,
A Triumphant Woman.

TODAY

I don't need you
to complete me.

My heart pieces
are now in synch
drinking champagne
in Le Marais

Love a la carte
I feel as loved
As I can remember.

You see,
when my heart sings,
it has nothing to do
with what we were or did,
such freedom of being.

No need to daydream now
As fortune embraces me
In the melodies
 of Edith Piaf,

I am no longer
begging
for your love
as a welcome dinner.

Walking down Rue Jarente,
Freedom & I
A song once sang
Loving melodies of life.

Today,
I don't need you to complete me.

Open your heart
to the wonders
that live within you.

Close any door
that takes you away
from seeing with your
soul's eyes.

Home

When I finally found my home,
with an outdoor patio to
   watch eucalyptus trees
   as oracles,
breathe well-being in
   the afternoon
   & converse with
my aging dog
   as a wizard,

your love came from the front door
and kissed me
showed me an open house
   & sold it to me in puzzle pieces.

When I finally found my home,
I saged it every morning
Palo santo it
Sprinkled it with
Indian incense,
daily prayers
and mantras-
even a little
lavender.

Never did I imagine
happy days
would have your scent

and my heart would know
how to peacefully stay.

Happy days in the Palisades.

You and I
have healed together.

We found each other in little pieces
and our love put us together,
restoring our illness into
Paraíso.

Yes, Paradise
that's the name of our house
& our street leads to
Via de La Paz,
The road to peace,
That's the name of our street.

What an irony because you and I
never really had a chance to experience
 Calm
- until now-

And here we are
tasting life
as we finally dance,
after going through so much.

Never did we imagine love could be
this warm.

YOU KNOW WHAT'S
REVOLUTIONARY

Tending to yourself
like it was the last day and
everyone's life depended on
the way
you raised yourself
as a flag of peace,
the way you stand for those in need.

Not leaning on someone's else life
to justify the way
 you did not live
your own time of this earth,

Taking,
Ticking away,

Someone is not to rob others
of their
only taste of being here,
not your parents,
 children or friends,
no one should strip you
of your finite life.

You know what's revolutionary

Arresting racism,
division,
greed & addiction

Savoring
TODAY,
That's all we can truly take.

Loving at every hour of the day,
Not just reserving it for
Your Holy- days
being in the present
in your beloved arms,

Amor
Taking it all in
that's nature's way,
today could be your last day.

You know what's revolutionary

Raising children to be less self-involved
and caring about the world,
less self-entitlement
more Service to ALL

You know what's revolutionary

Worshipping the earth
which sustains us,

Mother nature's love
Every day
She gives
&
We take

Let's refuse to hurt it more,
This is our home.

You tell me what's revolutionary!

WHEN WOMEN BECOME FREE

I wished I had told you
that I am an artist,

I can't just cook,
clean and conceive,
I don't want to grow old
without living my greatest dreams,

It is something I was born with
inside of me.

Yes, I have crazy dreams!

I want a build an all-female commune
for all of us,

WOMEN

to be free

For all our mothers and grandmothers,
who stayed married
because that was the only way
to dream
of financial stability,

the ones that had children
as their only way to be loved
and retain their lovers,
the ones surviving abuse
because it is easier to stay

than to claim their own throne.

·   How would it look like? - you asked.

It would have high ceilings,
 balconies to watch the stars,
tea rooms where we can all laugh and cry,
a dance club for womanly rites of passage,
dogs &
Rare flowers,

 Friendly trees
&
A crystalline river

Soulful music.

Artists of all kinds,

 Wild & Wise,

Irreverent,

Outspoken

Quiet & centered muses

to bring the right kind of balance.

A salon for best friends in life,
those we miss more than our romance,

The ones that get you,
feel you and don't hate you.

The crazy ones for when you are down,
and the wises one when you need a change of destiny
or lover,
&
the motherly ones
for all the open wounds

-There you have it- I said it.

To which you quickly replied with your eyes open wide:

-How much is this going to cost us?

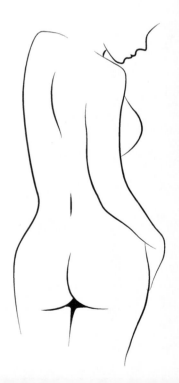

POETRY

I thought I had lost you,
not in the dramatic
type of way.
Not clothes thrown
over the window,
No!

You left me quietly
and I did not even
notice it,
my mind occupied
with everyday life-
making a dime.

I thought I had lost you
like I did myself,
for so many days

But you are a
Loyal love
Like a mother's touch,
never quite gone.

You came back through my fingers,
with a different kind of sweetness,

You welcome me,
sat me down,
pen on hand,
typed pages on
computer screens,
phone notes.

You made yourself apparent,
you could even say more
"imposing,"
more "I'm here to stay,"
kind of attitude.

You said:
nothing is going to separate us,
from now on
we are going to stick together,
never make anything else
a priority,

We are going to make each other a promise,
pinky fingers over a fire,
hold each other's amulets,
a soulmate's necklace.

From now on,
whoever comes
between us,
Even if it is our own
selves,

We are going to fight them
 until the end,
love claws onto walls,

I say:
Nothing
No one
Will come between us.
I finally listened.

I knew from very early on,
who you were,
who you are,
nothing
no one
as loving
as Loyal,
as life saving
like you,

Poetry,
Poesía.

Book

I'm a book.
I fly with the wind,
yet
I am strong
& happy.

I have not seen
busier days in ages
when people isolate
they
remember me.

Yet,
I'm not going to lie,
I would love to be at the beach
on a holiday,
drinking a piña colada,
soaking myself in coconut oil,
vacaciones

I wish I could fly
Travel the world
and pierce through

old libraries' windows,
then make someone
write about us,
immortalize us.

I guess,
It worries me
the stories
inside of me,
will die unread,
untouched.

And I would like others to
see me as a friend to soothe
their souls,
imagine other's world,
fantasize about true love.

How would I like to be
remembered?
As that "thing" that made you
A better Human.

Let's be a light to
each other's hearts
as we remember
our way home.

Once we arrive,
let's walk barefoot,
smell the flowers
& feel the presence
of all things good

Prevail.

HE TELLS ME NOT TO SIT ON THE SAND BECAUSE IT IS WET FROM THE RAIN,

I tell him I want to feel the moistness of the earth
 sit on it,
have it hold me
melt in it,
get dirty
go back to my roots.

He runs away from life,
I want to be right in the middle of it
taste it,
not leaving
 a color of it
unpainted.

THE GIFT

Living is enough.
Watching the sweetness of my chest raise with each breath-
that perfect cadence of creation.

Tides breaking within and sunsets sliding under my feet:
Every living moment where tranquility is offered: take it.

It is a gift from your creator.

Ask the ones locked in their darkness seeking purity of mind,
Ask the forgotten breathing in pure nostalgia,
Ask the pain stricken,
Lost in the verge of hopelessness.

Every living moment peace is offered:
Take it as a gift.

Ask the ones in detox centers and hospitals,
The ones behind bars and tortured,

Ask the ones fleeing from war or famine,
The heartbroken picking up what's left of their bones.

Every waking moment when dreamy stillness is given-
take it and plant it your heart,
this is a world where we need
to sweetly surrender.

It is a gift from your creator.

WRITE YOUR
OWN POEMS

If love had a name it would be...

_____

_____

_____

_____

_____

_____

_____

_____

_____

_____

_____

_____

_____

_____

Your love is a gift...

_____

_____

_____

_____

_____

_____

_____

_____

_____

_____

_____

_____

_____

_____

I am...

_____

_____

_____

_____

_____

_____

_____

_____

_____

_____

_____

_____

_____

_____

_____

Love is just a mirror pointing me to my own direction...

_____

_____

_____

_____

_____

_____

_____

_____

_____

_____

_____

_____

_____

_____

_____

_____

My gift...

_____

_____

_____

_____

_____

_____

_____

_____

_____

_____

_____

_____

_____

_____

_____

_____

I feel whole when...

_____   _____

_____   _____

_____   _____

_____   _____

_____   _____

_____   _____

_____   _____

_____   _____

_____   _____

_____   _____

_____   _____

_____   _____

_____   _____

_____   _____

_____   _____

Was it worth it?...

_____

_____

_____

_____

_____

_____

_____

_____

_____

_____

_____

_____

_____

_____

_____

_____

I am writing my own story...

_____

_____

_____

_____

_____

_____

_____

_____

_____

_____

_____

_____

_____

_____

_____

Davina Ferreira

Davina Ferreira is a poet, speaker and entrepreneur, founder of Alegría Bilingual Media & Publishing, a digital and multimedia company that connects the world with LatinX content via creative writing & storytelling.

The Alegría bilingual platforms include Alegría bilingual magazine, Alegría Mobile Bookstore, a traveling bookmobile that brings the joy of reading to younger generations in their own neighborhoods; and Alegría Video Series, a compilation of interviews with outstanding Latinx arts and culture figures. Alegría also creates live events featuring brand activations for creative artists & brands seeking to connect with emerging talent.

Ferreira was born in Miami but grew up in Colombia. She is the quintessential symbol of the immigrant's American Dream. Upon arriving in the U.S. Ferreira attended college, receiving a B.A. in Fine Arts from UC Irvine and worked as an actress at with the Bilingual Foundation of the Arts. Later on, she attended The Royal Academy of Dramatic Art in London (RADA) to pursue classical acting.

Ferreira then completed a Journalism Certificate at UCLA Extension and began a career in journalism, which led her to launch ALEGRÍA Magazine. She then wrote her first book, *Take Me With You/Llévame Contigo*, a bilingual compilation of short stories and poems of love. Years later, she wrote *Finding My ALEGRIA*, an inspirational memoir, which she hopes will motivate young entrepreneurs around the world to pursue their dreams regardless of their circumstances.

Ferreira has received The Rising Star Award, given to an entrepreneur under 35 by the prestigious National Latina Business Women Association, and the Latina of Influence Award by Hispanic Lifestyle magazine. This year, she received the CSQ Magazine New Gen Award for entrepreneurs under 40 at the Rockefeller Center in New York City.

She is also a sought-after speaker; whose passion is to inspire others to succeed as entrepreneurs. This Year, she has just returned from speaking at Harvard's Latina Lead Conference & Google's Women's summit.

Recently, she attended The Paris Writer's Retreat organized by Wendy Goldman & The Community Literature Initiative based in Los Angeles and founded by Hiram Sims.

If Love Has a Name is her first poetry book.

LET'S CONNECT:

You can connect with us and bring our live poetry show *If Love Had A Name* to your school, event or non-profit organization:

IG @davifalegria
davina@alegriamagazine.com

Your book purchase & spoken word bookings help us support our mission to bring the beauty of diverse poets to the world via our Alegría Mobile bookstore & the poetry classes we teach to underserved youth.